This Boxer book belongs to

....

For Ben,
without whom . . .

BOXER BOOKS and the distinctive Boxer Books logo are trademarks of Hachette Book Group, Inc.,
Carmelite House, 50 Victoria Embankment, London, UK, EC4Y 0DZ
Hachette Ireland, 8 Castlecourt Centre, Castleknock Road, Castleknock, Dublin 15, D15 XTP3,
Republic of Ireland; e-mail: info@hbgi.ie

© 2026 Alexandra Milton

All rights reserved. No part of this publication may be reproduced, stored in a retrieval system, or transmitted in any form or by any means (including electronic, mechanical, photocopying, recording, or otherwise) without prior written permission from the publisher.

This edition first published in Great Britain in 2026 by Boxer Books.
ISBN 978-1-4547-1283-1 (hardback)
ISBN 978-1-4547-1284-8 (paperback)

A catalogue record of this book is available from the British Library.

Boxer Books titles may be purchased in bulk for business, educational, or promotional use.
For more information, please contact your local bookseller or the Hachette Book Group's Special Markets
department at special.markets@hbgusa.com.

Printed in China

2 4 6 8 10 9 7 5 3 1

11/25

unionsquareandco.com

Quantity and weights of animal poo will depend on all sorts of factors such as size, sex, life stage, reproductive stage,
as well as many other things such as temperature of environment and calorific content of food.
The figures used in this book are approximations and not definitive.

Fact checked by Matthew Rendle RVN Veterinary Nurse,
chair of the Association of Zoo & Exotic Veterinary Nurses (AZEVN).

Whose Poo?

Alexandra Milton

Boxer Books

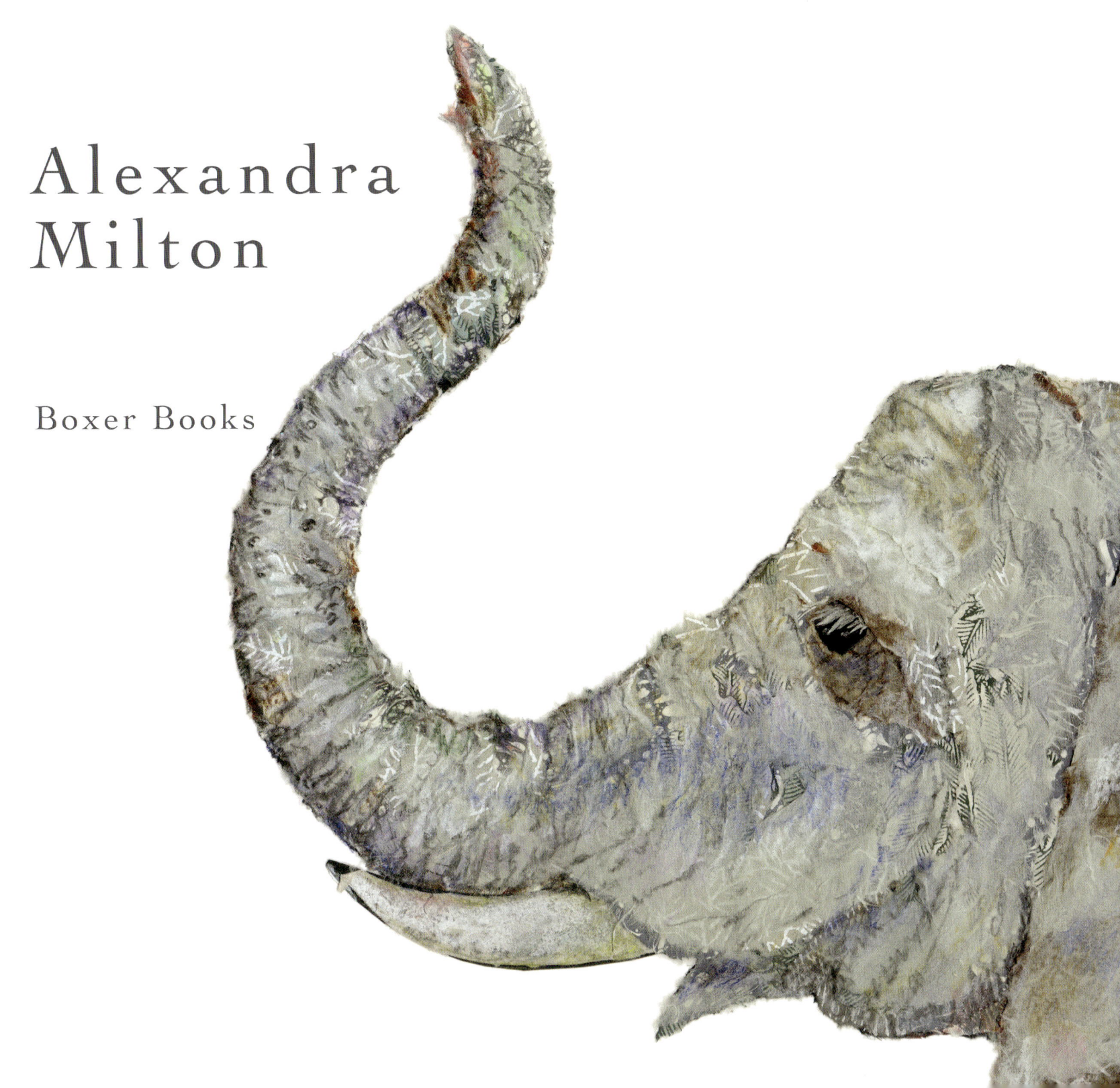

All lumpy and brown
and sprinkled with seeds.

Who did that poo?
Was it *you*?

It was this long-tailed monkey!

These little monkeys – called Emperor Tamarins – help replant the forest by pooing out the seeds of fruit they have eaten. These seeds then grow into new shrubs and trees. Monkey poo is the size and shape of an acorn.

Swishing and swirling
and floating like a cloud.

Who did that poo?
Was it *you*?

It was this brightly coloured parrotfish!

Parrotfish use their sharp teeth to scrape at coral that is covered in algae. They grind it up in their tummy, digesting the algae and releasing the coral as white sand. Each year, one parrotfish produces 450kg of sand – the weight of about four baby elephants.

White and runny
and sticky as glue.

Who did that poo?
Was it *you*?

It was this thin-legged stork!

Storks poo on their legs. The poo is often liquid when it is mixed with wee. As the wee evaporates, it cools the bird's legs. It also leaves behind a white powdery substance that reflects the sunlight and prevents the legs from getting sunburned.

Shaped like cubes
and stacked in a heap.

Who did that poo?
Was it *you*?

It was this big hairy wombat!

Wombats produce cube-shaped poo approximately two centimetres square. These little towers mark their territory with the shape of the poo preventing it from rolling away. Wombats can do one hundred poos a night.

These pellet-shaped droppings contain a surprise.

Look at them closely – there's an egg in disguise.

Who did these poos?
Was it *you*?

The poo is from the antelope and the egg is from the bird!

These antelopes are known as impalas. They find out about each other by sniffing at their droppings.

Little courser birds protect their eggs from being eaten by other animals by laying them next to the antelope poo. Both poo and eggs are the same size and shaped like olives.

WOW!
Who did *that* poo?
It *can't* have been you!

It was this *enormous* elephant!

Elephant poo is called dung and is the size and weight of a coconut. Elephants produce the equivalent of one hundred coconuts each day. Fresh plants are not good for baby elephants so they eat the digested plants in the poo produced by their mother.

Tamarin

Stork

Wombat

Antelope

Elephant

Other books in the Nature Revealed! series:

Shortlisted for the UKLA Book Award 2024

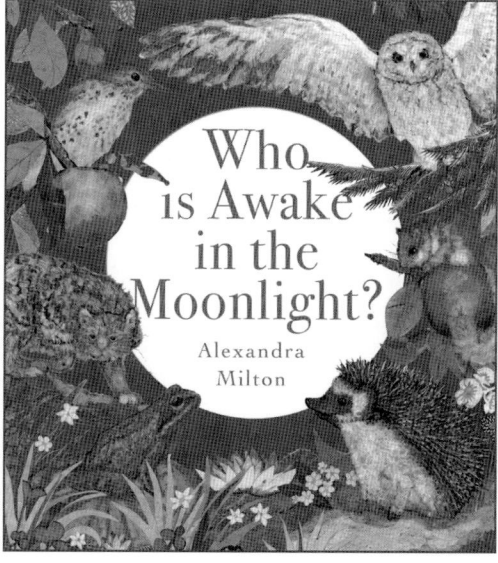